T0413430

Who Was Catherine the Great?

by Pam Pollack and Meg Belviso
illustrated by Dede Putra

Penguin Workshop

For Mike Volfman, computer genius,
tech entrepreneur—PP

Александру и Евгению—самым
терпеливым россиянам—MB

Dedicated to my Queen—DP

PENGUIN WORKSHOP
An Imprint of Penguin Random House LLC, New York

If you purchased this book without a cover, you should be aware that this book is stolen property. It was reported as "unsold and destroyed" to the publisher, and neither the author nor the publisher has received any payment for this "stripped book."

Penguin supports copyright. Copyright fuels creativity, encourages diverse voices, promotes free speech, and creates a vibrant culture. Thank you for buying an authorized edition of this book and for complying with copyright laws by not reproducing, scanning, or distributing any part of it in any form without permission. You are supporting writers and allowing Penguin to continue to publish books for every reader.

The publisher does not have any control over and does not assume any responsibility for author or third-party websites or their content.

Text copyright © 2021 by Pam Pollack and Meg Belviso.
Illustrations copyright © 2021 by Penguin Random House LLC. All rights reserved.
Published by Penguin Workshop, an imprint of Penguin Random House LLC, New York.
PENGUIN and PENGUIN WORKSHOP are trademarks of Penguin Books Ltd.
WHO HQ & Design is a registered trademark of Penguin Random House LLC.
Printed in the USA.

Visit us online at www.penguinrandomhouse.com.

Library of Congress Control Number: 2021932037

ISBN 9780399544309 (paperback) 10 9 8 7 6 5 4
ISBN 9780399544323 (library binding) 10 9 8 7 6 5 4 3 2 1

Contents

Who Was Catherine the Great? 1
A Good Marriage 7
A Whole New World 17
A Lonely Life 30
An Uncertain Future 45
The New Emperor 56
The New Empress 63
War and Plague 72
The Return of Peter the Third 80
Journey Down the River 87
The Last Empress 94
Timelines 106
Bibliography 108

Who Was Catherine the Great?

In early February 1744, much of Russia was covered in snow. A small village sat beside the best-kept road in the entire country. It was called the "winter highway." Empress Elizabeth used it to travel between Russia's two most important cities: Moscow and the capital, Saint Petersburg. One afternoon the villagers heard hoofbeats. Thirty grand sledges—fancy sleighs with enclosed compartments—were arriving in the village, pulled by horses. The people could tell that this was a royal procession heading to Moscow.

The drivers stopped to change their horses. They would trade the horses that were tired from the journey for new ones.

The villagers whispered to each other. Who were the passengers? Not Empress Elizabeth. She was already in Moscow with the Grand Duke Peter. Peter's sixteenth birthday was just a few days away. Rumors in Russia were that the empress had secretly invited someone to Moscow to become his wife.

When the carriages stopped, some of the villagers caught a glimpse of a young girl. She was fourteen years old, slim, with chestnut-colored hair and blue eyes. She was quiet, but looked around curiously as if this new country fascinated her. She was traveling with her mother.

"It is the bride of the grand duke," they thought.

The girl in the carriage was named Sophie. She was traveling east from the country of Prussia.

Her parents were noble people, but not royalty. And yet, it seemed as if the empress of Russia had chosen her to marry the heir to the throne.

On the evening of February 9, Sophie and her mother arrived at the Golovin Palace in Moscow. The castle was lit with flaming torches. Sophie unwrapped the furs that had kept her warm on the long trip. She was dressed in a

rose-colored silk gown trimmed with silver. She smoothed her dress and her hair. Then she stepped into the palace and waited to meet Empress Elizabeth and her future husband, the Grand Duke Peter.

On this night she was still Sophie of Prussia. Soon after, though, she would be given a new name: Catherine. She would adopt Russia as her own country and work to transform it into one of the most powerful nations in the world.

The people of Russia would grow to love her. They would call her Catherine the Great.

CHAPTER 1
A Good Marriage

Sophie Friederike Auguste von Anhalt-Zerbst was born on May 2, 1729, in Stettin, a military town in Prussia. Sophie's father was Prince Christian August von Anhalt-Zerbst. Although he was called prince, his family was not so very important. His wife was Princess Johanna Elisabeth of Holstein-Gottorp, a highly respected family in Prussia, which was an important part of the German empire.

Prince Christian was much older than Princess Johanna. She had wanted a life filled with fun and pleasure, but her husband gave her none of those things. When Sophie was born, Johanna was disappointed that she had not had a son. So when Sophie's brother, William,

was born eighteen months later Johanna gave most of her attention to him, sometimes ignoring her daughter, until young William died of scarlet fever.

After the loss of William, Johanna often went to visit her wealthy relatives and took Sophie with her. She even took her to the court of Frederick II, the king of Prussia.

The Holy Roman Empire

The Holy Roman Empire was not a country, but a group of European kingdoms, cities, and regions, each with their own leaders. Charlemagne, king of the territories now known as France, as well as of the Lombard people (one of several Germanic tribes), was crowned emperor of the Holy Roman Empire in the year 800. At different times the empire included parts of what are now the countries of France, Germany, Italy, Switzerland, Austria, and Poland—Germany being the largest.

This empire lasted until 1806, during the reign of Napoleon Bonaparte.

As a young princess Sophie knew that her job in life was to marry a rich man from an important family. Johanna wanted Sophie to make a good impression on the Holstein-Gottorp family. She made sure her daughter learned to dance and play music. She spoke German, which was the language of Prussia, and French. When Sophie visited her relatives she listened very closely to everything the adults said. She learned all about the important families in Europe. Sophie also carefully watched her mother. Johanna liked to brag and to be the center of attention. Sophie could see that this type of behavior made her mother unpopular, and she did not want to follow her example.

Sophie learned that her uncle had been named the guardian of the orphaned Duke of Holstein-Gottorp, eleven-year-old Karl Peter Ulrich, called Peter. He was the grandson of Peter the Great, the former emperor of Russia. When

Sophie met Peter he was a thin, delicate boy with blond hair. He was very shy and lonely and a little unpleasant, but Sophie was kind to him.

When Sophie was twelve years old, Russia got a new ruler: Empress Elizabeth. Elizabeth's father had been known as Peter the Great. She was not married and had no children. So she declared that Peter Ulrich, her orphaned nephew, would be her heir—the person who would rule Russia one day as Peter III. Elizabeth invited Peter to leave Prussia and live with her as part of the Romanov family in Russia.

Empress Elizabeth

Peter III

On January 1, 1744, Sophie's family sat down for a New Year's Day dinner. A courier arrived unexpectedly. He had a letter for Johanna. It was from Saint Petersburg. Johanna tore it open immediately. "The Empress Elizabeth," the letter announced, "desires Your Highness, accompanied by your daughter, to come to Russia as soon as possible." The letter said that Johanna would understand the "true meaning" of the request.

And Johanna certainly *did* understand it. Sophie, now fourteen, had been chosen to marry the future emperor of Russia!

CHAPTER 2
A Whole New World

Sophie's father was not invited to travel to Russia. She and her mother would make the journey in secret, using different names, because Empress Elizabeth didn't want anyone to know her plans. The journey to Russia in January was very hard but Sophie had no fear. She was excited about her future. They traveled in a heavy carriage over bumpy, frozen roads. Sometimes Sophie's feet got so cold she had to be carried out of the carriage because she couldn't walk.

At that time, the countries of Europe thought of Russia as an old-fashioned, even backward country. It was very large—the largest country in the world, spread over both Europe and Asia, but much of it wasn't yet developed. It contained grasslands, forests, mountains, and even near-deserts. Its citizens were uneducated. Many were serfs, the farmworkers who legally belonged to the people who owned the land where they lived and worked.

At the border of the Russian Empire the women traded their plain carriage for an imperial sledge. It was like a tiny house on runners that was pulled by ten horses. Inside, the windows had red curtains trimmed with gold and silver. It had quilted featherbeds with silk and satin cushions.

When they reached Moscow, Empress Elizabeth was waiting with Grand Duke Peter to greet them. Empress Elizabeth was tall. Her blond hair was dyed black. She wore an enormous hoopskirt trimmed with gold lace, and a glittering diamond necklace. Peter was still a thin, sickly boy. He was happy to meet Sophie, probably because she was not only his own age but spoke German like he did. Peter did not like living in Russia and stuck to his Prussian language and customs.

Sophie devoted herself to studying the Russian language. Her family was Lutheran, but she would have to convert to the Russian church to marry Peter. So she also studied the rituals of the Russian Orthodox Church. Sophie took all of her studies very seriously. At night she walked the hallways of the palace barefoot, in her nightgown, practicing her Russian vocabulary and grammar. It was a difficult language to learn. Russian even had a different alphabet than Sophie's native German.

The Russian Alphabet

The Russian alphabet is sometimes called the Cyrillic alphabet. It was created in the ninth or tenth century by St. Cyril, who traveled to Eastern Europe to spread Christianity. It has thirty-three letters. Some look and sound like letters in the Roman (Western) alphabet. Others look and sound completely different. Russia, in Russian, looks like this: **Россия**. **Р** is pronounced like the letter R in English. The **О** is pronounced like the O in "cross." **С** is like the C in circus. **И** and **Я** are entirely new letters, pronounced "EE" and "YA." So **Россия** is pronounced Ross-EE-ya.

Аа	Бб	Вв	Гг	Дд	Ее	Ёё	Жж	Зз	Ии	Йй
a	b	v	g	d	e	jo	ž	z	i	j
[a]	[b]	[v]	[g]	[d]	[ye]	[yo]	[ž]	[z]	[i]	[y]

Кк	Лл	Мм	Нн	Оо	Пп	Рр	Сс	Тт	Уу	Фф
k	l	m	n	o	p	r	s	t	u	f
[k]	[l]	[m]	[n]	[o]	[p]	[r]	[s]	[t]	[u]	[f]

Хх	Цц	Чч	Шш	Щщ	Ъъ	Ыы	Ьь	Ээ	Юю	Яя
x	c	č	š	šč	'	y	"	ė	ju	ja
[x]	[ts]	[tç]	[š]	[ç]	silent	[ɯi]	silent	[e]	[yu]	[ya]

It was so cold in the hallways where she practiced at night that Sophie got sick with pneumonia. Empress Elizabeth sat by her bed and sometimes held Sophie in her arms as if she were her own child. People at court worried that Sophie would die. Johanna wanted to bring a Lutheran pastor to comfort her daughter. But young Sophie asked for the priest who was her Russian Orthodox teacher instead. She already knew what would please Empress Elizabeth.

Although Sophie didn't know it, news of her illness was the talk of Moscow and beyond. Her chambermaids knew that she'd gotten sick by studying Russian late at night. They told the other servants, who passed the news around the palace

and out into the city. Soon everyone was praying for the foreign princess who loved their country so much. She seemed to be nothing like Peter, who only spoke German, as he had in Prussia, and didn't like his new country at all.

In April, Sophie recovered. She appeared at court for the first time on her fifteenth birthday. She still looked pale and thin, but she discovered that while she was sick many people had come to respect and even to love her.

Elizabeth quickly moved forward with plans for the wedding. Then disaster struck. Elizabeth found out about letters that Johanna had been sending to the king of Prussia. In the letters she talked about trying to get Elizabeth to get rid of her vice-chancellor. The Prussian king wanted him replaced with someone who was friendlier to Prussia. The letters showed that Johanna was a spy.

Sophie was terrified that she would be sent home, but Elizabeth didn't hold her mother's crimes against her. She allowed Johanna to stay in Russia until her daughter's wedding. Then she would have to leave.

On June 28, 1744, Sophie was baptized in the Russian Orthodox Church. She recited her Orthodox vows by heart in Russian. She was given a new Russian name, Ekaterina, or "Catherine" in English. Catherine was now ready for her marriage. But before the wedding could take place, Peter became very sick with smallpox—a disease that created fluid-filled bumps on the skin, like blisters, that grow and burst. People who survived the illness were often scarred for life.

When Peter finally recovered, his face was horribly scarred. Catherine was determined to show that she didn't care what Peter looked like. But the first time she saw him after his illness, without meaning to, she winced. Peter was a very resentful boy. He never forgave her for making him feel ugly, even if it was by accident.

From then on Peter would never be her friend. But on August 21, 1745, he became her husband.

CHAPTER 3
A Lonely Life

Catherine never forgot how kind Empress Elizabeth had been to her when she was sick. But Elizabeth was not always so nice. As the empress, Elizabeth was used to being able to do whatever she wanted. If she was in a bad mood or Catherine displeased her in any way, she would punish her. She also wanted complete control over the new couple. If any lady-in-waiting became too friendly with Catherine, Elizabeth would send her away.

When Catherine's mother went back to Prussia, she left behind a lot of bills that had not been paid. Catherine vowed to pay her mother's debt with the allowance that Elizabeth gave her. This was almost impossible because Catherine had plenty of expenses: gifts for people at court and her own fancy wardrobe. Her title was now "Grand Duchess," and she had to live up to her new role.

Life in a Royal Court

A royal court is usually made up of a ruler—like a king, queen, or emperor—and the people who work closely with the ruler. Members of the court are considered an important part of the household, and they hold many different jobs, including bodyguard, musician, and teacher. Some are

called ladies-in-waiting or gentlemen-in-waiting. These people are usually close friends or relatives of the ruler. Every court reflects who the ruler knows best, and who they trust the most.

In order to do well and be successful at court, a person has to learn the same traditions, manners, and fashions as the other people in the royal circle of friends.

Elizabeth was very impatient for Catherine and Peter to have a baby who would rule Russia after Peter. But Peter did not treat Catherine like a wife. He wasn't very nice to her. Catherine had to listen for hours while he played the violin, badly, or talked about himself. At night, Peter took out armies of toy soldiers. He arranged them all over the bed and acted out imaginary battles while his young wife yawned from boredom.

A few weeks after the wedding, Peter announced that he was in love with one of Catherine's ladies-in-waiting! There was nothing Catherine could do about it. As time passed,

Peter became interested in many young women at court but never his own wife. Everyone in the court knew that Catherine was being ignored by Peter.

Catherine felt even more alone when she got news from home in March 1747 that her father had died. Because he was not royalty, she was only allowed to wear her mourning clothes—black dresses—for six weeks. She was then expected to attend parties and balls even though she was very sad.

Catherine spent much of her time reading. Now that she had learned Russian, she read every Russian book she could find. She also read French. She especially liked the work of philosophers of the Enlightenment. Without the help of any teachers, Catherine was educating herself.

One thing that always seemed to make Catherine happy was riding horses. At that time, women usually rode sitting sideways on their horse. Empress Elizabeth insisted that Catherine ride that way. But Catherine liked to ride very far and fast and she couldn't do that while riding sidesaddle. So Catherine invented a secret saddle that could change positions. She always left the stable riding sidesaddle. Once she was out of sight, she changed the saddle, swung her leg over the side, and galloped away.

Age of Enlightenment

The Age of Enlightenment describes a historical period between the seventeenth and eighteenth centuries. Before this time, no one questioned why a king had more rights than a slave. People started to champion the rights of ordinary citizens. When Thomas Jefferson wrote, "We hold these truths to be self-evident, that all men are created equal . . ." in the Declaration of Independence, he was echoing the ideas of the Enlightenment.

Many other modern values, ideas, and methods of scientific discovery had their start during this time, which is sometimes also called the Age of Reason.

In 1751, Empress Elizabeth assigned three young noblemen to be Peter's gentlemen-in-waiting. One of them was Sergei Saltykov. Sergei really liked Catherine and tried to convince her to be his girlfriend. He was very handsome and

charming. They often went riding together. Even though they were married, Peter didn't seem to care if Catherine knew about the other young women he liked. So finally Catherine agreed to be Sergei's girlfriend.

In 1754 Catherine became pregnant. Many people knew that Sergei was the baby's father. But since she was married to Peter, the baby would still be heir to the throne. On September 20, 1754, at the summer palace in Saint Petersburg, Catherine had a son. Both Catherine and Peter acted as if the baby was Peter's son.

No one was happier about the baby than Empress Elizabeth. She had never married and never had a child herself. She swept into the room, named the baby Paul, and had him bathed and wrapped up. Then she left the room and ordered the nurse who helped deliver the baby to follow her—with baby Paul. Catherine was left alone. She quickly realized that Elizabeth wasn't going to give the baby back! As far as the empress was concerned, this was *her* baby. Once again, there was nothing Catherine could do.

Seventeen days after Paul was born, Elizabeth gave Sergei Saltykov the important mission of announcing to other countries that Peter and Catherine had had a baby who was the heir to the throne. He was to leave immediately for Sweden. After that trip he would be assigned to go to Hamburg, a city-state that was part of the Holy Roman Empire, to be a Russian representative there.

Sergei would not be coming back to Russia. Catherine was alone again.

CHAPTER 4
An Uncertain Future

Catherine took her role as grand duchess very seriously. But she still wasn't treated well. Now that she had a son who was heir to the throne, she decided to demand more respect. Instead of being shy, she began speaking to whomever she wanted to. She stopped worrying about what Elizabeth thought. She became close friends with the British ambassador and the Russian vice-chancellor. She impressed them with her knowledge and intelligence. These men came to see that Catherine would be a better ruler than her husband, Peter, or even Elizabeth herself. But even talking about this was a very dangerous idea. Plotting against the current ruler was a crime.

One nobleman that Catherine spoke with often was the Polish secretary of the British ambassador. Stanislaw Poniatowski briefly became Catherine's boyfriend before he was sent back to Poland. Together they had a daughter, Anna, in 1757. But the baby did not live very long. She died when she was only fifteen months old.

A year earlier Prussia had invaded its neighbor, Saxony, bringing Russia into the Seven Years' War. Great Britain was on the side of Prussia. Russia, under Elizabeth's orders, sided with Austria.

The ongoing war made Empress Elizabeth suspicious of some of her advisors. She thought they were plotting against her. In 1758 she had the vice-chancellor of the Russian Empire, Alexey Bestuzhev-Ryumin, arrested. Elizabeth had found letters that he had written to Catherine. In them,

he wrote about the war. Even worse, Bestuzhev said that he wanted Catherine to become empress after Elizabeth died.

Catherine was terrified. Would Elizabeth arrest her, too? She decided to ask Elizabeth for a private meeting. The empress didn't answer her for two months. Finally, she had Catherine brought to her bedroom in the middle of the night. When Catherine got there, Peter was with the empress. Catherine could see a judge behind a screen. She realized that at that moment in the royal bedroom, she was on trial. If she was found guilty of treason—the crime of betraying her country—she would be arrested.

Catherine threw herself at Elizabeth's feet. She hoped she could make Elizabeth care about her the way she had when Catherine was so sick. Catherine cried about how lonely she was, insisted that she had never been disloyal, and begged for Elizabeth to send her home to Prussia.

She did not want Elizabeth to be angry at her son, Paul, if she was found guilty.

Elizabeth softened. Peter was furious. He hoped to get rid of Catherine and marry his latest girlfriend. He angrily claimed that Catherine was lying. But Elizabeth was annoyed at his rudeness. She declared Catherine innocent and sent her back to her room. Catherine was saved.

Even though she was Prussian, Catherine was completely loyal to Russia in every way. But Peter made no secret of the fact that he was still loyal to Prussia. As the war continued, he openly celebrated whenever Prussia scored a victory against Russia. He also gave the king of Prussia any secret information he could to help him beat Russia in the war. *This* was treason. He was expected to consider Russia his home the way Catherine did. But Peter was betraying the country he would one day rule.

The Seven Years' War 1756–1763

The Seven Years' War involved all the great powers of Europe, as well as the Americas, West Africa, India, and the Philippines. In Europe, two opposing sides were led by Great Britain and France, who were fighting over colonial boundaries in

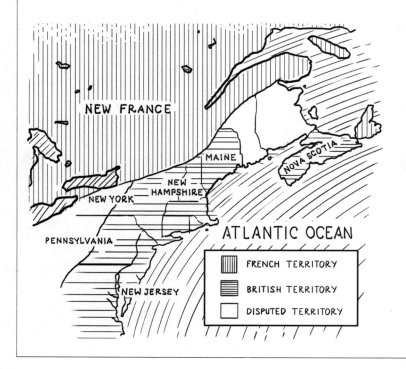

North America. When other countries saw Great Britain and France were going to have a war, they were either pulled into the conflict or jumped in hoping to get something for themselves. The war ended with the signing of the Treaty of Paris and Treaty of Hubertusburg.

Empress Elizabeth's health was getting worse, and Peter often bragged that as soon as she died he would make sure that Russia was friendlier to Prussia. Catherine hated to think of her adopted country being ruled by someone who didn't love it the way she did. She couldn't help but imagine all the things she would do if she were empress herself. She wanted to make Russia even more powerful than it already was.

Some of the Russian soldiers resented Peter's attitude. But they respected Catherine. One soldier in the Imperial Guard caught Catherine's attention, handsome Grigory Orlov. He was one of five soldier brothers who were all loyal to Catherine. Shortly after meeting Grigory, Catherine fell in love with him.

Grigory Orlov

On January 3, 1762, Catherine and Peter were called to Elizabeth's bedside. She was dying. Although Elizabeth wasn't always kind to her, Catherine cried at the idea of losing her. Two days later, Elizabeth died. She was fifty-two years old

and had ruled Russia for twenty-one years. Peter would now become the emperor and his wife, Catherine, would be the new empress consort. Catherine and Russia could only wait to see what happened next.

CHAPTER 5
The New Emperor

Empress Elizabeth's body was laid out in her coffin in the Cathedral of Our Lady of Kazan in Saint Petersburg. For ten days, Russian citizens walked by the coffin to say goodbye to their empress. Through it all, Catherine knelt on the floor of the church, in mourning. Peter showed no such respect. He was busy throwing parties to celebrate becoming emperor. The Russian people noticed these differences.

Peter told everyone his plans for Russia—and they weren't popular. He immediately ended the war with Prussia, a country most Russians by now considered the enemy. He gave Prussia back territory that Russia had won in the war. He also abandoned Russia's allies, France and Austria.

He wore a Prussian military uniform and forced the army to dress the same, taking away their warm Russian coats. He planned to convert the Russian Orthodox Church to the Lutheran faith. He even bragged that he planned to divorce Catherine, send her to a convent, and then marry his girlfriend.

Prussian uniform

Catherine, with the Orlovs' help, hoped to rule instead of Peter. But she couldn't act right away.

She was pregnant with Grigory Orlov's baby. If Peter knew this, he would have even more reason to divorce her. So she decided to wear her fullest mourning dresses.

On the night her baby was born, April 11, 1762, a trusted servant set a fire outside the palace. Peter rushed outside. That gave Catherine enough time to give birth to her son, Alexei, in secret. Before Peter returned, the baby was bundled up and taken away to be raised in safety by one of Catherine's servants. At the end of that month, Peter ordered Catherine to attend a banquet to celebrate the new alliance with Prussia. Although Catherine was still his wife, Peter sat at the head of the table with his girlfriend. Catherine was seated far away.

Peter then moved Catherine to Peterhof, an estate in the country. He and his girlfriend moved to a bigger and fancier home. Now Catherine could only wait. Who would come for her first? Peter, to send her to a convent, or the Orlovs, to tell her it was time to capture Peter so Catherine could replace him as ruler of the country?

On June 28, 1762, Catherine was awakened at dawn by Alexei Orlov. All was ready. He brought Catherine to the army barracks in Saint Petersburg where the soldiers kneeled in front of her. They wanted her as their empress.

Next, they went to Kazan Cathedral where the Russian Orthodox archbishop declared her empress in the eyes of the church.

Catherine—along with an army of soldiers—marched to the Winter Palace. Catherine announced that her husband had betrayed the Russian people, and she would become their ruler to save the country.

The time had come to deal with Peter. Catherine dressed herself in a military uniform to ride to the house where Peter was. Soldiers offered pieces of their own uniforms for Catherine to wear as she led the march. On the way there, a messenger rode up with a note from Peter. He had heard that he had been overthrown and would no longer be the emperor. At first he offered to share the honors of ruling the country with her, but then he begged Catherine to let him return to Prussia with his girlfriend.

Catherine would not agree to either of those things. Instead, she ordered her soldiers to guard him closely at an estate outside of Saint Petersburg. She sent his girlfriend to Moscow.

Peter had been emperor of Russia for six months. But when Catherine made her move, as the king of Prussia later said, Peter "allowed himself to be dethroned like a child being sent to bed."

CHAPTER 6
The New Empress

Catherine was going to be empress of Russia. But the way she came to power raised a lot of questions. Elizabeth had not named her the heir. She wasn't related to the Russian royal family like Peter and her son, Paul, were. As long as there were other people who might have had a stronger claim to the throne than she did, Catherine knew that someone else could try to be named ruler of Russia.

On July 6, 1762, only a week after Peter had been captured, Catherine received a letter from Alexei Orlov. Peter was dead. How he died was a mystery. Catherine knew that she would be accused of ordering Peter's death. She told people he died of natural causes, and then she displayed his body so everyone could see he was really dead.

Catherine was crowned empress on September 22, 1762, at the Kremlin in Moscow. She wore a dress made of silver brocade trimmed with fur, and she sat on a diamond throne. Her crown had forty diamonds, each an inch across, surrounded by many smaller diamonds, thirty-eight pearls, and an enormous ruby. It weighed nine pounds.

The Kremlin

Kremlin is the Russian word for "fortress." In medieval times, there were hundreds of them in Russia. Today there are only about twenty. The most famous is the Kremlin in Moscow. It sits in the middle of the city, overlooking the Moscow River. Some parts date back to the fourteenth century.

The Kremlin is not just a single building. It includes five palaces, four cathedrals, and a palace where the Russian king, called a tsar, once lived. Today it is the residence of the Russian president. It is also a museum that draws millions of visitors every year.

Catherine was ready to put her plans into action. She knew that Russia was deeply in debt. The country had borrowed a lot of money during the war, most of it from banks in Holland. The soldiers in its army had not been paid in months. Catherine announced that she would not take the allowance that every empress was paid. Instead, she put that money—her own salary—back into the national treasury. Each day she woke up at five or six o'clock and worked for fifteen hours. She studied everything she could about what was happening in Russia.

In the past, Russia's government had been filled only with people from important families. But Catherine sought out the brightest people she could find from any background and gave them important jobs. She invited people from all over Russia to elect representatives to come to Moscow and talk about what was most important in their own regions. It was the first time Imperial Russia tried to give its people a voice in their own government. Catherine hoped to make better laws for her people. A French philosopher named Denis Diderot was so impressed with her that he started referring to her as Catherine the Great, and soon others did, too.

Catherine also wanted to show the rulers of other European nations that Russia had a rich culture. In 1764 she commissioned an architect to build a modern palace that she filled with a large collection of impressive paintings. She called it the Hermitage.

The Hermitage

The Hermitage is the second largest art museum in the world. It was founded in 1764 and celebrates its birthday every year on December 7, Saint Catherine's Day. It is made up of six buildings, including the Winter Palace where the royal family sometimes lived. Originally,

very few people were allowed inside. (The museum gets its name, Hermitage, from the word "hermit," a person who lives alone.) But it has been open to the public since 1852.

Today the State Hermitage Museum collection contains more than three million works of art and artifacts from prehistoric times right up to the modern age.

Catherine wanted to improve the lives of ordinary people in Russia, and so she established many schools. One of the most famous was the Smolny Institute for Girls. Catherine made regular visits there and supervised the lesson plans. She wanted other girls to have the kind of education she had given herself. She ordered

hospitals to be built. She wanted Russian doctors to learn all the latest scientific treatments. But one thing that Catherine wasn't able to do was change the lives of Russia's poorest people, the serfs, those who were owned by the same person who owned the land on which they lived and worked.

Catherine believed in the ideas of the Enlightenment. She wanted to encourage free speech and a free press in Russia. She thought that slavery, the death penalty, and torture were all wrong. And she wanted the serfs to be freed. But this was easier said than done. If Catherine freed all the serfs, the noble families of Russia and the church, both of whom owned many serfs, would turn against her. In 1762 serfs were free labor to wealthy landowners. And even an empress couldn't change a country overnight.

CHAPTER 7
War and Plague

Now that she was empress, and a widow, many people expected Catherine to marry again and to have more children. Some thought she would marry her boyfriend, Grigory Orlov, which made people jealous of the Orlovs. They thought Grigory marrying Catherine would give his family too much power. Because the Orlovs weren't royal, some people even plotted to kill Grigory!

Another possible husband for Catherine was her old boyfriend Stanisław Poniatowski. He hoped that Catherine would call him back to Russia so they could be together. But Catherine didn't want to marry anyone. She wanted to rule Russia alone. She knew that Stanisław could be useful, though. She wanted to make him the king of Poland. Because kings in Poland were elected by the people, Catherine gave him money to campaign for the job. Stanisław won the election.

Russia was far larger and more powerful than Poland. Stanisław always seemed to need money, which Catherine provided. In this way, she knew he would always be loyal to her. Holy Roman Emperor Joseph II of Austria, Catherine's ally against Prussia, agreed with her plans to keep Poland friendly.

Many people in Poland objected to what they saw as Russia taking over Poland, and rebelled. Catherine sent forty thousand Russian troops into Poland to fight them. When the Russian soldiers chased the rebels across the Polish border into Turkey, Turkey declared war on Russia.

Catherine hoped that if she fought a war with Turkey, she could win control of Crimea, an area that extended to the Black Sea.

This would give Russia year-round ports for its navy. (The ports Russia already had froze over during the winter.) In 1770, Russia and Turkey fought a battle at sea. Russia destroyed fifteen out of sixteen Turkish ships. Nine thousand Turkish seamen died—and only thirty Russians. The Russian navy had been led by Grigory Orlov's brother Alexei.

Other European countries were surprised and impressed with Russia's success. They were also afraid. What if Catherine decided to expand the Russian borders and take over their countries, too? They weren't interested in starting a new war.

Catherine didn't want to fight, either. She agreed to a meeting with Joseph II of Austria and King Frederick II of Prussia.

Frederick came up with a deal to satisfy all three countries. They would divide about a third of Poland's land between them. Catherine would take the Eastern part, an area known as "White Russia" that was populated by people of the Russian Orthodox faith. Today it is the country of Belarus. Frederick took an area of thirteen thousand square miles with six hundred thousand people who mostly spoke German and were Protestant. Joseph II took a big part of southern Poland, which was mostly Catholic. Poland's king, Stanisław, agreed with whatever Catherine wanted. The Polish people were shocked and angry. Many vowed never to allow Poland to be divided again.

Joseph II of Austria

Russia now stretched all the way to the Black Sea. But the war had come with an unexpected cost. Soldiers who had been fighting in Turkey brought home a disease called bubonic plague when they returned to Russia.

King Frederick II of Prussia

Bubonic Plague

The bubonic plague is a type of bacteria in the blood. An outbreak in Europe in the fourteenth century killed 60 percent of Europe's total population. People then did not know what caused the disease, but we now know it was spread by fleas that were carried on rats who traveled on ships. People with the plague got swollen glands called "bubos." The disease was also called the Black Death because the skin of the victims sometimes turned black before they died. Today we use antibiotics to fight the bubonic plague.

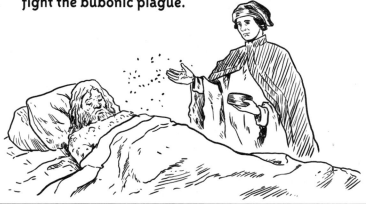

Within months, nearly one thousand people were dying every day in Moscow. Bodies lay rotting in the street. They couldn't be buried fast enough. People were so scared they blamed doctors for bringing the plague and refused to follow their advice.

Catherine saw Moscow slipping out of her control. What could she do? In her hour of need, her old friend Grigory Orlov offered to take over. He gave strict orders to the people of Moscow: They had to obey their doctors. He ordered them into a quarantine—which meant that the sick stayed isolated from the healthy. This kept the disease from spreading. He burned houses and clothing that were infected and had the bodies cleared away. Grigory was forceful but kind. The Russian people saw that Grigory was trying to save them.

By December the death count had fallen dramatically. Moscow survived the plague. Catherine awarded Grigory a gold medal for saving the city.

CHAPTER 8
The Return of Peter the Third

On October 1, 1772, Catherine's son, Paul, turned eighteen. Catherine immediately started to search for a bride for him. She hoped to have a grandchild who would be heir to the throne after Paul.

Paul and his mother did not get along. Because he'd been taken away from her as soon as he was born, she had never really been able

to grow close to him. Paul greatly admired the memory of the father he barely knew, Peter III. He started imitating everything he had ever heard about him. That included wanting to be Prussian and admiring the Prussian king. This did not make Paul popular with the people at the Russian court. It made Catherine doubt if he should one day become emperor at all.

Then, in September 1773, a man pretending to be Peter III appeared! His real name was Yemelyan Pugachev. He had served in the cavalry until he ran away from the army to the Russian province of Orenburg. This part of Russia was still very wild and unsettled. Here Pugachev was joined by thousands of followers who came from the different peoples that lived all over this area south of Moscow.

None of Pugachev's followers had ever seen the real Peter III. They didn't know what he looked like. Pugachev told them that *he* was the true emperor of Russia. He said that Catherine had tried to have him killed because he was going to free all the serfs. But he had escaped.

In the rural region of Orenburg, Pugachev threw himself into playing the role of emperor. He wore a scarlet caftan and velvet cap. He held a scepter in one hand and a silver axe in the other.

He granted titles to his friends, naming them after real people at Catherine's court. His followers made their own gold coins to use as money. Because he couldn't read or write he had a secretary write down his orders and sign them: "The great sovereign, the Russian Tsar, the Emperor Peter the Third." Whether or not his followers really believed he was Peter III, they liked what he stood for. He encouraged them to rise up and kill their wealthy landlords.

Back in Moscow, Catherine dismissed Pugachev as a troublemaker and sent one of her generals with a small force to capture him. But she had underestimated the size and power of his rebellion. By 1774 Pugachev had more than fifteen thousand followers! Catherine was afraid.

Catherine sent more soldiers to fight the rebels. This time Pugachev ran away. He disappeared into the Ural Mountains with about two thousand of his followers in March 1774. Four months later, in July, he reappeared, having gathered a force of twenty thousand more people. This time the Russian army defeated him and he was captured.

Pugachev was brought to Moscow in an iron cage. He was executed on January 10, 1775. Catherine pardoned everyone else involved in the rebellion. But it made her believe even more that Russia needed a tough ruler—that's what she had to become.

The following year Paul married a Prussian princess, Sophie, who took the name Maria Fyodorovna. They had a son, Alexander. Catherine would never have taken her grandson away from his mother the way Paul had been taken from her. She was determined to love her grandson.

CHAPTER 9
Journey Down the River

Paul and Maria soon had a second son, Constantine. Catherine loved spending time every day with her grandchildren. They kept her from becoming too sad when she received the terrible news that her loyal friend Grigory Orlov had died. He left all his money to the son he had with Catherine, Alexei.

Grigory Potemkin was now Catherine's boyfriend. In 1783 Catherine sent him south to the Black Sea. She hoped to gain even more land for Russia—including the important city of Constantinople—to make Russia the largest empire in the world. Potemkin was successful and claimed the Crimean Peninsula for Russia. Although Catherine was now their leader, she did not try to force Russian customs on Crimea.

Potemkin met with the people in the peninsula. In Catherine's name he built towns, churches, and shipyards. Catherine wanted to celebrate her new territory and her expanded power. Potemkin organized a trip for her down the Dnieper River. He invited other world leaders to join her as Catherine toured her empire. Joseph II of Austria accepted the invitation and became the first European ruler to ever visit Russia.

Catherine started her trip in 1787, traveling in fourteen luxury sleighs complete with carpets, couches, and tables. The big sleighs were followed by many smaller sleighs full of servants, hairdressers, musicians, and even silver polishers. At every stop on the journey cooks went ahead to prepare great feasts.

The sleighs carried the party to the city of Kiev where they boarded boats complete with music rooms and libraries.

The voyage was a great success. But the rulers of Turkey saw Catherine as a threat to their territory. They knew she wanted to invade Constantinople. In August 1787, the Turks once again declared war on Russia. Catherine trusted Grigory Potemkin to defend the country. She named him supreme commander in chief of the Russian army in the south. Soon after that the Swedes also declared war on Russia, hoping to win territory in the north.

Two years later, Sweden admitted defeat. Catherine thought the Turks would soon give in as well. Potemkin was in Saint Petersburg where Catherine was celebrating her sixty-first birthday. Catherine asked him to go back to Crimea to meet with Turkish ambassadors to discuss peace. As always, Potemkin wanted to serve her well. But he had gotten sick with malaria nearly a decade earlier. Along the way to Crimea, he felt too ill to continue. He scribbled one last note to Catherine: "Gracious Sovereign, I can no longer endure my torments."

Potemkin was helped out of the carriage so he could lie on the earth of the country he loved. There he died. Back in Saint Petersburg, Catherine was shocked when she got the news.

In January 1792, Catherine signed a peace treaty with Turkey. Although Russia had not won Constantinople, it had gained more new territory. But it didn't feel like a victory without the man she loved by her side. "Who could ever replace Potemkin?" she asked over and over. "Whom shall I rely on now?"

CHAPTER 10
The Last Empress

When Catherine was crowned, many people thought she would not hold the throne for long. But by 1796, she had been empress for thirty-five years. She was sixty-seven years old. She had dealt with uprisings and wars, but her throne remained secure.

Catherine had grown stout in her old age. Her hair was snowy white. She wore glasses and used a magnifying glass to read official documents. Her beloved greyhounds slept in a basket beside her bed.

She still got up at six o'clock every morning. She answered letters while drinking her morning coffee. Then she met with ministers, generals, and other government officials about government business. Catherine still encouraged anyone she spoke with to give their own opinions and tell her if they thought she was wrong about something.

In the afternoon, she always had lunch with friends. Then she read, sewed, or embroidered.

Every day her grandsons visited her. When Alexander and Constantine arrived, Catherine stopped whatever she was doing and got down on the floor to play with them. She read to them, told them stories, gave them hugs, and played games like blindman's buff. Her grandsons said that their games were "never so merry" as when their grandmother played with them.

Catherine took charge of the boys' education. She made sure that Alexander had an English nanny and that he learned all about European history. Constantine's nurse was Greek, and he was taught the history of Greece and Rome. These choices made it clear that Catherine had plans for her grandsons. She wanted Alexander to be the emperor of Russia. His younger brother, she hoped, would rule Constantinople one day. She still didn't believe that her own son, Paul, was the best choice to be ruler at all.

Catherine also had ideas for how the boys should be raised. She wanted them to plant and to grow their own gardens. If they were scolded, it was in private. If they were praised, it was in public. "I praise loudly. I blame softly," she said.

Paul and Maria had several daughters, but Catherine did not spend as much time with them. In July 1796, they had a third grandson, Nicholas.

On November 16 of that same year, Catherine woke up as usual and had her coffee. Then she went into her dressing room. A long time passed, and she still hadn't come out, even when the servants knocked. Finally they pushed open the door. Catherine was lying on the floor. They carried her to bed. Paul, Maria, and their children all rushed to her bedside. She had had a stroke. Catherine the Great died on November 17, 1796.

Paul was quickly crowned emperor of Russia. One of his first acts as ruler was to enact a law that only the eldest son could inherit the Russian throne. Catherine became the last woman to rule Russia.

Catherine is still considered one of the greatest leaders Russia ever had. During her reign, Russia became the most powerful empire in the world. She expanded its borders to include Crimea and the Black Sea, which gave the country a much-needed warm-water port. The new cities of Kherson, Nikolayev, and Sevastopol were built during her reign. Others, like Saint Petersburg and Odessa, were improved or redesigned.

She built hospitals and made sure that doctors were well educated. Thanks to her, millions of Russians were protected against smallpox and other diseases that had killed many people in the past.

She created schools to educate both girls and boys.

She also created one of the greatest collections of art, bringing works from all over Europe to Russia. Her grandsons added many more treasures to it after she died. Russia, which had a reputation as a very old-fashioned country, became a center of culture and philosophy.

Bartolomé Esteban Murillo's *Walpole Immaculate Conception*

When Catherine first arrived in Russia as a young girl, she wasn't sure what her future might bring. Never willing to let other people decide her fate, she made her own plans. She conquered the Russian language, the Russian throne, and the hearts of the Russian people. She earned her place in history and her title—Catherine the Great.

Timeline of Catherine the Great

1729	Catherine the Great is born May 2, in Stettin, Prussia
1744	Becomes engaged to be married to Karl Ulrich, Grand Duke Peter of Russia, heir to the Russian throne; travels from Prussia to Russia with her mother
1745	Marries Peter on August 21
1754	Catherine's son with Sergei Saltykov, Paul, is born
1762	Empress Elizabeth Petrovna Romanov dies, and Peter becomes emperor of Russia
	Seizes the throne from her husband, Peter, and is named empress of Russia
	Catherine's son with Grigory Orlov, Alexei, is born in April
	Catherine's husband, Peter, dies on July 17
1764	Begins building the Hermitage
1768	Is vaccinated for smallpox and encourages Russians to do the same
1770	Russia wins territory that stretches to the Black Sea in war with Turkey
1787	Catherine tours her empire, including taking a boat trip down the Dnieper River
	Catherine makes Grigory Potemkin commander in chief of the Russian army
1796	Catherine dies November 17, in Saint Petersburg

Timeline of the World

- **1729** — The Comet of 1729, possibly the largest comet on record, is sighted in Nimes, France
- **1732** — Laura Bassi becomes the first female physics professor at the University of Bologna, Italy
- **1737** — The oldest existing English-language newspaper, *The Belfast News-Letter*, is founded in Ireland
- **1742** — Anders Celsius creates the Celsius temperature scale
- **1743** — The last wolf in Scotland is shot
- **1755** — Samuel Johnson publishes *A Dictionary of the English Language*
- **1756** — Wolfgang Amadeus Mozart is born in Salzburg, Austria
- **1776** — The Declaration of Independence is written in Philadelphia, Pennsylvania
- **1783** — The volcano Laki in Iceland begins an eight-month eruption
- **1785** — Jean-Pierre Blanchard and John Jeffries become the first people to cross the English Channel by air in a balloon
- **1792** — US Postal Service established
- **1796** — Jane Austen begins writing *Pride and Prejudice*

Bibliography

*Books for young readers

Anirudh. "10 Major Accomplishments of Catherine the Great of Russia." Learnodo Newtonic, May 24, 2017, https://learnodo-newtonic.com/catherine-the-great-accomplishments.

Collins, Cynthia. "Hermitage Museum: Catherine the Great's Legacy to Russia." **Guardian Liberty Voice**, February 20, 2014, https://guardianlv.com/2014/02/hermitage-museum-catherine-the-greats-legacy-to-russia.

Maranzani, Barbara. "8 Things You Didn't Know About Catherine the Great." History.com, July 9, 2012, https://www.history.com/news/8-things-you-didnt-know-about-catherine-the-great.

Massie, Robert K. **Catherine the Great: Portrait of a Woman**. New York: Random House, 2011.

*Vincent, Zu. **Catherine the Great, Empress of Russia (A Wicked History)**. New York: Scholastic, 2009.

*Whitelaw, Nancy. **Catherine the Great and the Enlightenment in Russia**. Greensboro, NC: Morgan Reynolds Publishing, 2005.

Website

saint-petersburg.com